A Knight's Journey

Carole Wilkinson

sundance
A Haights Cross Communications Company

🐾 a black dog book

Published by Sundance Publishing
P.O. Box 1326, 234 Taylor Street, Littleton, MA 01460
800-343-8204

Copyright © text Black Dog Productions

First published 1999 as Phenomena by
Horwitz Martin
A Division of Horwitz Publications Pty Ltd
55 Chandos St., St. Leonards NSW 2065 Australia

Exclusive United States Distribution: Sundance Publishing

ISBN 0-7608-8037-9

Printed in Canada

Contents

Author's Note

I've always loved stories of King Arthur and his knights. There's something very appealing about those stories. I enjoy reading about gallant knights in armor galloping off on horses, leaving their ladies to await their return.

However, when I was researching this book, I learned the truth about the lives of real knights and medieval women. Life in a castle with little heating and no glass in the windows must have been chilly. A diet of meat and bread doesn't sound too exciting either. The facts and the fiction about knights don't quite match.

Carole Wilkinson once worked as a laboratory technician. She decided that wasn't much fun. So now she writes books for children and teenagers instead.

Introduction

CLOSE YOUR EYES and try to picture a knight. Most likely he will be covered from head to foot in shining armor and charging along on his horse. If you picture him at home, he will be living in a castle, probably somewhere in England.

There is a way to find out if our picture of a knight is true. We can look back through historical records and at paintings of the time. We can read the tales of King Arthur and his Knights of the Round Table. How do the knights of history compare to our image of a knight?

What we find is that our image of a knight is nothing like a real knight. Knights were around for about 600 years. The way they lived, the armor they wore, and the enemies they fought changed over time. In the beginning, real knights weren't much like our imagined knights at all.

Let's follow the story of knights and their ladies. Through history we can find out where facts became fiction and fiction became facts.

Chapter 1: Introduction

Imagine . . .

being a soldier in the English army ready to fight invading Normans in 1066.

SELWYN HAD a good view from his place on Senlac hill. He could see the Norman army below. There were plenty of soldiers, but he wasn't afraid. Their archers had already tried to attack and failed. Hundreds of arrows had been shot. But the wall that Selwyn and his fellow soldiers made by standing their shields next to each other protected them. Arrows either stuck in the shields or fell to the ground. Once their arrows were used up, the archers hurried back to the shelter. But not before a few English arrows had found their mark in Norman flesh.

Selwyn got ready for the next attack. He settled his helmet on his head, checked his supply of lances, and shifted the shield on his arm. He was ready for whatever the Normans could hurl at him.

The enemy soldiers surged forward. Selwyn and his companions rushed toward them with a yell. Their lances flew through the air and found their mark in many Normans. When Selwyn had used all of his lances, he pulled his battle-ax from his belt. He kept advancing, waving the huge ax before him. The Normans began to panic and then retreated. Selwyn and his companions charged after them, waving their axes and yelling insults about their cowardice.

Selwyn saw his commander shouting something at the troops. He tried to stop and hear what he was saying. But the soldiers behind him pushed him on as they all rushed downhill after the cowardly Normans.

"Look, the enemy is bringing in more men," Selwyn yelled to the man next to him. "They've just arrived."

He pointed his ax toward a group of Normans riding

toward them on horseback. He stood fast, ready to face this new batch of enemies. They would be just as easily scared off as the other Normans. His companions stood ready beside him. They waited for the soldiers to get off their horses and face them in combat. But the Normans didn't get off their horses. They kept riding. They rode around the English soldiers. What were they doing? Selwyn realized that the soldiers on horseback had cut off their retreat. They couldn't get back to their commander and the rest of the English forces up on the hill.

The Normans still didn't get off their horses. Instead they turned their horses and ran them straight at the English foot soldiers. They hurled their lances as they rode. Selwyn and his comrades couldn't understand what was happening. When the mounted soldiers ran out of lances, they drew their swords. Surely now they would get down off their horses and stand ready for battle. They didn't.

They continued to charge on their horses, knocking down English soldiers as they sped by. The confident yells of the English turned to shouts of fear. They looked back to the distant safety of the hill. More soldiers on horseback were attacking the rest of the English troops. Was that King Harold knocked to his knees by one of the fearsome warriors?

One of the mounted warriors looked straight at Selwyn. He spurred on his horse and headed straight for him. Selwyn had his ax ready, but the warrior's sword flashed before his eyes. The sword crashed into Selwyn's chest. He fell to the ground, and his enemy struck him again. Selwyn tried to get to his feet but couldn't. The mounted warrior turned and charged back. He looked like a terrible demon—half-man, half-horse. The demon bore down on him, nostrils steaming, sword swinging, and the world went black. . . .

Chapter 1

Wayward Warriors

THE EVENTS IN this story took place during the Battle of Hastings on October 14, 1066. It is one of the best known battles in history. Selwyn was an English soldier trying to protect his country from the invading Normans.

The Norman invaders were the first knights in England. English soldiers rode to battle on horses. But they got off their horses and tied them to a tree before they started fighting. The Normans fought on horseback. This gave the Normans a great advantage in battle.

At first, the English defeated the Normans in several battles. But the combination of the mounted soldiers backed up by archers and foot soldiers finally proved too strong. The English king was killed, and the country was taken over by the Norman army—all in one day.

Norman: A person who lived in the area called Normandy in northwest France.

The Knights

Long ago, knights were soldiers who fought with hand weapons on horseback. They protected themselves from enemy weapons by wearing armor. Knights were the most important soldiers in Europe for more than 600 years.

Knights lived and fought during the Middle Ages, or the medieval period. It lasted roughly from 1000 A.D. to 1600 A.D.

Knights first appeared in France. The early knights didn't ride off in search of adventure. Being a knight was their job. It was how they earned a living.

Early knights were often uneducated and violent. They protected the land of their lord against attack from neighboring lords.

At that time, there was no government in charge of the entire country. There weren't many laws, and there were no police. Any arguments were settled with the sword.

armor: A covering used to protect the body in battle.

Basic Equipment

At first, anybody could become a knight. All a man needed to call himself a knight was a horse, weapons, and some armor.

However, this equipment was very expensive. This meant that only men who were quite rich could afford to become knights.

Chain Mail

Chain mail was made up of small rings of iron wire. The rings were flattened out and riveted, or joined, together to form chains. Then the chains were riveted together to make a metal fabric. If someone tried to stab a knight, the chain mail stopped the blade from cutting his flesh.

The chain mail was made into a simple shirt-like garment called a hauberk. This was just a straight body covering with no sleeves. Selwyn and his enemies wore hauberks during the Battle

of Hastings. Only the upper body was protected. For added protection, the knight carried a very large kite-shaped shield. Made of wood covered in leather, the shield was big enough to protect most of his body.

What Was a Knight's Life Like?

In medieval times, land was owned by rich men called lords. Knights protected the lord's castle and land. In return for this service, the lord gave each knight a piece of land.

Sometimes the knight lived in his lord's castle. But usually he lived with his family in a house or a smaller castle on his own land. He had fields to grow food and keep animals. He also had servants to do the work for him.

The knight swore loyalty to his lord. He had to be ready to fight battles for him. If his lord had to travel, the knight would go along to protect him. The knight also had to spend about 40 days each year in the lord's castle.

What About the Ladies?

The lives of knights revolved around fighting. Their role as protectors of the land made them important. Women didn't fight. Their main role was to look after their homes and children.

The wives, sisters, and daughters of knights were called

ladies. Because they were from noble families, they were considered to be better than peasant women.

Most women in the Middle Ages didn't have much control over how they lived their lives. They were expected to do as men told them. Every lady was under the charge of a man. This could be her father, her husband, or her brother. If all of her male relatives were dead, a male guardian was selected to look after her.

In Service

A lady's childhood and any education she received prepared her for just one thing—marriage. A girl was often married by the time she was 14 years old. Her husband was chosen by her parents. If they could, they chose men who were rich and had lots of land. To attract a good husband, a girl's parents had to provide a gift of money and land called a dowry.

Any land or riches that a woman owned or inherited when her parents died did not go to her. These things went to her husband.

noble: Upper-class landholders who were usually rich.

peasant: Person of the lower class who did not own land but worked the land of a lord.

A lady had only one other choice besides marriage. She could join a convent and become a nun. Nuns gave their service to the church, but they still didn't have any real independence.

Women's World

The place where ladies did have power was in their homes. A knight's wife did not do any of the cooking or cleaning herself. Her servants did these chores. Her job was to organize the servants and tell them what they had to do. This was a big responsibility.

In the Middle Ages, people didn't buy many things. They had to grow most of what they ate. All of the food and drink for the family and the servants had to be prepared by the household. Clothes and bedding were hand sewn, mostly from material that was made at home.

The lady of the house organized all of these activities. She planned how much food to grow and then organized servants to prepare and preserve the food. They had to salt meat and fish for the winter. They had to store vegetables and grain. If the lady of the house didn't get these things right, her family and servants would go hungry.

When her husband was away fighting battles,

the lady had complete control of the household. If anyone attacked the castle, she had to organize the men to defend it.

History in Wool

The Bayeux Tapestry

Not very many books were written in medieval times. A lot of knowledge about this period comes from art. Some very detailed paintings and other art have survived that show us how people lived.

The most detailed information about the Battle of Hastings was not written down. It was sewn in wool.

As well as sewing useful things like clothes and rugs, women also made wall hangings called tapestries. The most famous of these is the Bayeux Tapestry. It shows scenes of events leading up to the Battle of Hastings and the Norman Conquest of England.

conquest: A battle in which an enemy is defeated.

18

The tapestry is only 20 inches deep but more than 230 feet long. It was made to be hung around the walls of a big room. It shows us exactly what Norman knights wore, what weapons they used, and how they used them.

A scribe

A team of unknown women embroidered, or stitched, the Bayeux Tapestry. The tapestry these women did was extremely important. It helped us to understand more about life during the Middle Ages.

Dark Ages

In the early Middle Ages, printing hadn't been invented. Books were written by hand, usually in Latin. Only rich people and priests learned Latin. Most people, including many knights, couldn't read at all.

The first English book that recorded some historical events of the time was called the *Anglo-Saxon Chronicle*. It was started in 890 A.D., and many unknown scribes continued writing it. Here is a translation of what was recorded about the Battle of Hastings:

"William the Earl landed at Hastings, on St. Michael's Day. Harold came from the north and fought against him before all his army had come up. And there he fell, and his two brothers, Girth and Leofwin. And William subdued this land."

It doesn't really tell us much at all. The pictures in the Bayeux Tapestry give us a much better idea of what happened.

Living by the Sword

By the end of the 11th century, knights were found all over Europe. But a man now needed more than a horse and a coat of mail to become a knight. In fact, at that time, only the sons of knights could become knights. Knights saw themselves as members of an exclusive club. They were a breed of men who lived for fighting. We think that peace is normal and that war is a bad thing. Knights thought that war was normal. Peace for them meant there was nothing to do. Without war, there was no way to prove how brave and skilled they were.

Imagine . . .

you are a young squire about to be knighted in Normandy in 1167.

FOR AS LONG as he could remember, William Marshal had waited for this day. He had been training and practicing for 13 years.

He and his fellow squires had started the ceremony the night before. They had all bathed to cleanse themselves of their sins. Then they had spent the whole night in the church praying.

William had fallen asleep at one point, but no one seemed to notice. Now the sky to the east was starting to turn a rosy pink. He slowly unbent his aching knees and got to his feet. At last the day was dawning when William would become a knight.

The clothes he was to wear were laid out for him in his room. They were all new and in the bright colors that he liked. He was especially excited about the new scarlet robe. It had a leather hood and little gold lions embroidered around the edge. He would wear these splendid garments during a grand ceremony, which was to begin that morning.

His daydreams were suddenly disturbed. Panicked voices broke the silence.

"The enemy is at the gate. To arms!"

Sir Roger burst into William's chamber.

"Quick, young Marshal," he said. "Put on your battle clothes."

"But what about my ceremony?"

"You will be knighted immediately in the courtyard," said Sir Roger.

William quickly scrambled into his hauberk and other old garments. He pulled on his chain mail leggings, vest, and other protective clothes. Grabbing his helmet and his weapons, he ran out into the courtyard. The castle was in a panic. They had expected plenty of warning before an attack, but the

French king's men were already outside the castle. Sir William de Tancarville, the lord of the castle, was away at the border. Without him to lead them, no one seemed sure what to do.

"Kneel down in front of me," Sir Roger told William and the other squires.

The squires did as they were told. A priest quickly blessed their swords. Other knights came and strapped on their swords and their spurs. Sir Roger gave each squire a quick, light tap on the shoulder with his sword.

"Be thou a knight," he said to each one in turn.

The young men stood up, blinking as the sun's rays suddenly broke over them.

That was it. William was a knight. There was none of the ceremony and splendor that he had been imagining since he was a boy. It was all over in five minutes.

Now he had to go out and fight the enemy. William had no experience of war. There had been peace all through his squiring. The only people he had ever fought were other squires. This was not only his first day as a knight. It would also be his first day in battle.

William went to the stables to collect his new horse, a gift from Sir William, his lord. It was a handsome horse, chestnut with a white blaze above his nose. The animal munched peacefully on some fresh straw. Unlike William, the horse didn't know what was ahead of him. A servant came to help him get the horse ready for battle. He strapped on the saddle and adjusted the stirrups.

The poor horse had no protection against the enemy weapons. It didn't seem fair. William adjusted his chain mail coat. He was already sweating.

He mounted the horse and hoped he would fight well. He did not want to disgrace his lord or his family.

The servant led him out to the castle gate. Only the day before, that had been his job. He hoped he would be brave and not give way to fear. He also hoped this day would not be his last. . . .

Chapter 2

Knight School

WILLIAM MARSHAL needn't have worried. His first battle, in 1167, was very fierce, but he did well. His lance was broken at the very first charge. A French soldier pulled him from his horse with a big hook. William had a scar from the wound for the rest of his life. His new horse did not survive the battle, but William bravely continued to fight on foot with his sword.

But the older knights didn't praise William. Instead, they said he should have captured an enemy horse and weapons to replace the ones he'd lost. William hadn't been thinking about gaining anything for himself. He had been fighting hard to protect the castle. The older knights reminded him of what he must do if he wanted a career as a knight. He had to think about making a profit.

Like Father, Like Son

At the age of 20, William Marshal had just reached the end of his training to be a knight. His father was a knight, so he became a knight, too.

He didn't have a choice. His older brother would inherit his father's land and house. So William had to make his living as a knight.

All young boys destined to be knights spent the first years of their childhood at home. William was left in the care of his mother and the other ladies of the household. Around the age of 11, he began his training to become a knight. He was not trained at his own home. He was sent off to the castle of a rich uncle in Normandy. All knights' sons were sent away from their homes for training.

Page Boy

The first stage of learning how to be a knight was being a page. William Marshal was quite old when he started his training. Boys were usually sent away when they were seven years old.

A page was really just a servant. He had to do household chores like setting the table, serving food, carving meat, and lighting candles. He also learned how to ride a horse well. He played ball games with the other pages in order to get strong. Sometimes the young knights were taught how to read and write.

destined:
Meant to be.

Pages spent a lot of time with the ladies of the household. The ladies taught them songs and sometimes how to play a musical instrument. They also taught the young pages manners and how to behave.

From Page to Squire

When a boy turned 14 years old, he moved to the next stage of training—being a squire. He had to learn how to use a sword and a lance, both on foot and on horseback. Squires spent many hours each day doing a lot of physical training.

A squire was the personal servant of one particular knight. It was the squire's job to wake up the knight in the morning. He then helped him to dress and served him food. A squire also had to take care of the knight's horses, clean the stables, and look after the knight's armor. When the knight went to battle, the squire went with him.

Play Fight

The squires practiced fighting by fighting each other and by using some special equipment. One piece of equipment was called the quintain. This was a target shaped like a shield. The squire had to practice hitting the shield in the center with his lance. First he did this on foot, then on a horse. The shield wasn't fixed, though. It was suspended from one end of a pole that could swing around. On the other end was a weight. When the shield was struck, it swung around. The squire had to run or ride by quickly or he would be hit by the swinging weight.

This taught him to strike his enemy and then quickly get out of the way. This way the enemy couldn't strike back.

Another item used for practice was the pel. This was a padded wooden post that the squires used to practice their sword strokes. When they became skilled, they would practice with other squires.

The squire trained for at least six years before he became a knight. If a man couldn't afford the equipment to become a knight, he continued to be a squire.

Arise, Sir Knight

The ceremony to make a squire a knight was called dubbing. Dubbing ceremonies for early knights were very simple. But soon the Church became involved, and dubbing became a long ceremony. If William Marshal hadn't had to rush off to battle, his dubbing ceremony would have been much more splendid.

How to Be a Knight

A French knight called Geoffrey de Charny wrote a book called *The Book of Chivalry* in 1350. This book was like an instruction manual for knights. It told knights how they should behave. It described the special bath, the all-night vigil, and a dubbing ceremony that lasted for two or three days. The book told what the knight's clothes and equipment symbolized. The white surcoat meant that the knight must stay free from sin. The red shirt showed his readiness to shed his blood. The black hose, or stockings, on the legs represented the earth. They were a symbol that the knight was ready to die at any time.

vigil: A period of time spent watching or praying before a special event.

surcoat: A long vest worn over armor to protect it from rust.

Two older knights assisted in the ceremony, strapping a sword and golden spurs onto each new knight. Then they tapped them with their own swords on the back of the neck. This light blow on the neck was called the collée.

Here is what Geoffrey de Charny wrote about this ceremony:

". . . as the sword cuts on both sides of the blade, so should they (the new knights) defend and maintain right, reason, and justice on all sides. . . . Then the knights who confer the order should kiss them as a sign . . . that peace, love, and loyalty may be in them. Then these knights should give them the collée as a sign that they should forevermore remember this order of knighthood. . . ."

What Weapons Did Knights Use?

When a knight was ready for battle, he sat on his horse. His broad sword would hang on his right side in a special holder called a scabbard. Under his arm he carried a lance. On his left side was his shield and his battle-ax.

A knight's lance was an iron point mounted on a long wooden pole. The lance was normally 9 to 12 feet long. It was made from the wood of a yew or ash tree. This was the weapon that set a knight apart from other soldiers. If foot soldiers carried a lance, it was a shorter weapon that they threw. The knight never let go of his lance.

The knight's sword was big, a little over three feet long, heavy, and double-edged. He needed two hands to use it effectively. The sword didn't have a sharp point, but it had very sharp edges. It was used to slash rather than to stab.

The shield was carried on the left arm or in the hand. The knight used it to prevent the enemy's blows from striking his body.

When a knight was fighting in single combat with an enemy knight, his lance was of no use. If he lost his sword, he would rely on his ax to strike his enemy.

Another weapon used was a mace. This was a club with an iron head used for bashing the enemy. A mace sometimes had spikes or ribs.

Armor

With all of these terrible weapons used against him, how could the knight protect himself? If he didn't want to be stabbed, slashed, or bashed to death, he had to have better armor.

By the end of the 12th century, the knight was covering every part of his body with chain mail.

The tunic was longer, down past the knees. It now had long sleeves and a hood. The knight also wore chain mail leggings and gloves to protect his legs and hands.

Knightly Underwear

A knight could be struck by a sword, a lance, or an ax. His chain mail protected him from being badly wounded, but he could still get nasty bruises. Underneath the chain mail, the knight wore a padded vest called an aketon.

The knight wore iron plate pieces over his knees and elbows. He was now wearing a larger helmet called a helm. This was a flat-topped helmet. It went over the top of a padded cap and chain mail hood. This would have been the sort of armor that William Marshal wore. He was well protected. But he didn't look much like the knight in shining armor that we imagine.

A Knight's Best Friend

A horse was the most important part of the knight's equipment. The knight's warhorse was called a destrier or a charger. It was bred to be bigger and stronger than ordinary horses. It had to be able to charge at a gallop while carrying a knight with all of his weapons. The horse also had to be unafraid of the noise in a battle.

A good warhorse cost at least six times as much as a cow. If he could afford it, the knight would have two warhorses, in case one got wounded. He only rode the horse in battle and while he was training for battle. When he was traveling, he rode a smaller horse called a palfrey.

Inventions

Soldiers had been riding horses for centuries before knights existed. What made the knights different from these earlier mounted soldiers?

Knights used some of the modern inventions of the time. The most important of these was the stirrup. It was a metal loop that hung from each side of the saddle to support the rider's foot. Before stirrups were invented, a rider on a horse didn't have much control. He would slip around on the horse's back. Knights used stirrups on long straps and rode with straight legs. They also used saddles with a raised part at the front and back. This stopped them from slipping around. A knight could stand up in his stirrups and lean sideways without falling off his horse.

Another invention that helped the knight's riding was the horseshoe. With iron horseshoes nailed securely to its hooves, the horse was much more surefooted on rough and rocky ground.

A Coat of Plates

Even in the 14th century, the knight still didn't look much like our imagined "knight in shining armor." More armor was used, but you couldn't see much of it. What he wore was called a coat of plates. It consisted of small pieces of iron riveted on the inside of a sleeveless leather garment. A knight still wore a chain mail hauberk underneath this.

Other pieces of armor protected his arms and legs, but these were strapped on separately. The leather gauntlets that covered his hands had small metal plates. His helmet now had a visor, which he pulled down to protect his eyes and nose. Only a narrow slit remained for him to see through.

Now that he had more protection, the shield didn't need to be so big. The sword used by a knight became thinner and had a sharper point.

Full Armor

Not until the middle of the 15th century did knights begin to wear a full suit of armor. It wasn't all joined together, though. The front and the back plates hung from leather shoulder straps. Separate arm and leg armor was strapped on. At last, 500 years after his first appearance, the knight is in shining armor!

Shields became even smaller now that the knight was covered from head to foot in steel. Knights added daggers to their stock of weapons. They used them to stab their enemies in places that were unprotected, like the armpits.

Heraldry

When a knight wore full armor, it was impossible to tell who he was. So that everyone would know who was who on a battlefield or in a tournament, knights started wearing symbols. They wore these symbols on their surcoats and also on their horses' caparisons. The symbols became known as coats of arms. The knowledge and study of them is called heraldry. Knights later put

caparison: A decorated covering for a horse, especially a warhorse.

their coat of arms on everything from their shields to their dinner plates.

Men known as heralds kept records of the different symbols. They made sure that no two knights chose the same symbol. As well as keeping lists of coats of arms, heralds had other jobs. They made announcements at tournaments and carried messages.

Nowadays, descendants of knights and royal families still use their own coat of arms. Some countries, cities, and schools also have their own coat of arms.

Imported Armor

It was even more expensive than before for a knight to provide his own armor. It might cost a year's income. It needed to be specially made to fit his own body, and now he had to send overseas for it! Armor was no longer something that the local blacksmith could make. It was very complicated and needed an armor-maker specialist to construct it. The best armor-makers were in Italy, Germany, and Spain.

The armor was very carefully and cleverly made. Each piece was hinged and connected so that the knight could move quite freely. He could get on a horse, run, and get up if he was knocked down. All of this could be done while wearing full armor.

A full suit of armor weighed 44 to 55 pounds. It was very hot inside. It wasn't uncommon for a knight to suffocate inside his suit.

Fortunately armor didn't wear out! Also, if it was damaged, it could be repaired. Some young knights inherited armor from their fathers and grandfathers.

Armor was made from very smooth, polished metal. Every piece had a curved surface. This is so arrows would skid off unless they hit the armor at an angle of exactly 90 degrees. This meant that the knight was usually safe from arrows unless they were being fired from point-blank range.

suffocate: To die due to lack of air.

Chapter 3: Introduction

Imagine . . .

you are a knight in 1099 advancing with an army to the town of Ascalon.

BALDWIN FELT SWEAT trickling down his back. His white surcoat was doing little to reflect the terrible heat. His armor was almost too hot to touch. He felt like a baking chicken. The Egyptian army was spread out on the plain below. Baldwin had never seen such a big army in his entire life. There must have been 20,000 men. He looked back at his army gathered on the bare mountainside. They didn't number more than 2,000. His commander, Duke Robert of Normandy, didn't look a bit worried at the sight of such an army. If he was worried, he didn't show it.

"We may not have great numbers," Duke Robert told his men. "But what we do have is the advantage of surprise."

Baldwin strained his eyes at the camp below. Some of the enemy soldiers were preparing food while others were resting. They were not prepared for battle, and luckily, they hadn't seen the Norman army approach.

Duke Robert arranged his men in three columns. To their left were three more columns led by Duke Godfrey of Bouillon. To their right, there were another three columns under Count Raymond of Toulouse. The nine columns moved forward together. They advanced down the hillside to the plain below with banners flying and armor glinting in the sun. There was no one left in reserve for a second attack, since they didn't have enough men. If the first charge failed, the battle was lost. Baldwin was reminded of a saying his mother was fond of using. It was something about putting all of your eggs in one basket.

The activity in the enemy camp suddenly changed. The Egyptians started rushing around like disturbed ants, gathering up arms and getting ready for battle. Baldwin knew that the Egyptian lookouts must have seen them. The enemy was soon ready for battle. The first defenses carried bows and iron maces. Behind them were Egyptian foot soldiers armed with spears. At the rear were their horsemen, fearsome but not wearing armor like the knights.

There was a flash of light as the sun reflected on something shiny on the plain below. "Look," shouted Duke Robert. "There's al-Afdal's golden battle shield. I'll capture that prize or die trying."

He called out the battle cry. The knights charged toward the enemy while the archers fired arrows to protect them.

The knights gathered speed when they reached the flat plain. The Egyptian army started to make a terrible noise such as Baldwin had never heard before. They shouted out strange sounds, blew notes on trumpets, and banged drums. It was like the sound of a nightmare. It made the sweat turn cold on Baldwin's skin despite the terrible heat. The Egyptian archers suddenly dropped to one knee as they prepared to take aim. There was no turning back now. Baldwin charged with his lance under his arm. Around him his brother knights did the same.

The enemy's arrows might have been made of straw for all the effect they had. Before the archers had a chance to shoot again, the knights were upon them. When their lances were broken, they slashed with their swords. The enemy foot soldiers turned and ran in terror. The enemy army on horseback tried to circle behind them. But the knights on each side drove them back with ease. Baldwin could see the confusion in the eyes of the Egyptians as they ran away from him. . . .

Chapter 3

Battles and Crusades

THE BATTLE OF ASCALON, in 1099, was a brilliant victory for the knights of France. It demonstrated the power of well-armed and well-armored knights. The enemy army may have had ten times more men. But they were powerless against an organized cavalry charge. The Egyptian army was chased into the sea. This was the last battle in the First Crusade. More about the crusades will be discussed later in this chapter.

Battle Plan

Knights weren't the only soldiers fighting in battles. Usually about a quarter of the army were knights, and the rest were foot soldiers and archers. A battle often started with each army's archers firing arrows at each other. Sometimes a short clash would occur between the foot soldiers. Frequently the

cavalry: Troops mounted on horseback.

knights were saved until later. In Chapter 1, we learned that this happened at the Battle of Hastings. The knights always had support from their infantrymen. But it was the knights who often decided who would win the battle.

The knights usually fought in groups of 30 to 40 under one leader. Usually two or three of these groups would charge together. They rode as close together as they could. This meant that they attacked as if they were one unit, bristling with lances. They would ride right over the foot soldiers and fight the enemy knights.

The trick was not to be the first to charge. Often battles were lost because the knights charged too early. So each army had to try and get the other one to charge first. This battle plan did not change from the 12th to the 15th century.

Holding On

The knight charged at his enemy at high speed with his lance tucked firmly under his arm. He didn't throw his lance. He held onto it and hit the enemy with the full weight of himself and his horse. This style of attack was called using "a couched

bristling: Covered with many sharp, stiff points.

lance." He hit his target with such force that his lance could be knocked out of his grip. To stop this, a lance was made with a large metal disc near the end of the staff.

This disc would rest up against the knight's shoulder. When he hit his target, the disc pressed against his shoulder. This prevented the lance from slipping out of his grasp.

Who Were Knights' Enemies?

The early knights fought in Europe against local enemies who threatened to take the lands of their lord. If they served a lord who wanted more land, knights would have to attack neighboring lords to win their land.

Knights also fought wars with Muslim soldiers. Muslims from North Africa, called Moors, had invaded part of Spain. The knights who lived in Europe sometimes went to fight the Moors.

Muslim: Person who follows the religion of Islam. Most Muslims live in the Middle East, northern Africa, and southern Asia.

Crusades

A knight's job was to fight. It was what his whole life was about. When the pope called on knights to journey to the Holy Land to fight the Arab Muslims, many knights decided to go.

The pope didn't like the idea of Muslims taking over the places where Jesus was born and lived. Even though the knights had to pay for the journey themselves, they were very eager to go. They wanted to fight this powerful enemy. It was also an opportunity for younger sons of knights to go off and seek their fortune.

A number of lords gathered together an army of about 4,000 knights. They also took more than 20,000 foot soldiers. The army was mostly from France, but there were knights from Italy and Germany as well.

This great movement of knights and soldiers later became known as the First Crusade. Their aim was to take the holy city of Jerusalem back from the Muslims.

A Long and Winding Road

In 1096, the first crusaders set out to ride or walk to the Holy Land. This was a mammoth journey of 2,400 miles across lands that they knew very little about. It was not an easy journey. They had to cross mountains and deserts. The crusaders suffered from the terrible heat, thirst, lack of food, and sickness. Nothing about the Holy Land was familiar to them.

The knights were successful, however. After winning several battles, they took Jerusalem in July 1099. It had taken them three years to achieve their goal.

When the conquering knights finally broke into Jerusalem, they behaved in a very unknightly way. They killed everybody in sight—men, women, and children. Accounts at the time described the streets as being ankle-deep in blood.

Homesick

Now that the crusaders had taken Jerusalem, most of the knights returned home. Before they left Europe, many knights had thought of owning a piece of the Holy Land. But when they realized that the land was hot and dry, most of them went back home. Very few of them stayed in the Holy Land.

Some knights decided to stay and defend the newly conquered land. They wanted to protect any Christians who came to visit these holy places. If everyone left, Jerusalem and the other cities would soon be retaken by the Muslims.

Monk-Knights

In 1119, two French knights, Hugh de Payens and Godfrey de St. Omer, decided to form a special group of knights. These knights would stay in the Holy Land to defend it. They called the group the Order of the Templars. To be a member of the order, a knight had to obey strict rules. First, he had to be very religious and live very simply. He couldn't wear fancy clothes or own any personal possessions. And he was not allowed to marry.

The group thought ordinary knights were too interested in comforts and riches. The members cut their hair short but let their beards grow long. They lived much the same way as monks did, with strict rules for prayer and fasting.

fasting: Not eating for a certain amount of time.

These knights became known as the Knights Templar. Other orders of knights were also formed including the Knights Hospitallers and the Teutonic Knights.

Jerusalem Falls

Although the Templars and the Hospitallers fought very hard to defend Jerusalem, they couldn't keep it. After only 88 years in Christian hands, it was taken over by the Muslims again in 1187.

More crusades followed to try and retake Jerusalem. Over the next 100 years, there were six more crusades, but they all failed. Jerusalem remained in Muslim hands.

How Do We Know What Happened?

All of these things happened hundreds of years ago. Fortunately, one knight wrote down his experiences during the three years of the First Crusade. His book, written in Latin, is called *Deeds of the Franks (Europeans) and the Other Pilgrims to Jerusalem.*

This book was found in 1101, only two years after Jerusalem was taken. It has been used as a basis for history books about the First Crusade ever since. We don't know the name of the author. From what he said about himself in the book, historians have guessed that he was from southern Italy.

This unknown knight describes the difficult conditions of the crusades. He tells about pursuing the Muslims through a deserted, waterless land. He also describes how the crusaders suffered greatly from hunger and thirst. At one point, he wrote that they found nothing at all to eat except prickly plants.

Women at the Crusades

As well as knights and soldiers, ordinary people, including women, went on the crusades. The writer of the *Gesta* tells us how the women helped during one battle.

"The women in our camp were a great help to us that day. They brought up water for the fighting men to drink and gallantly encouraged those who were fighting and defending them."

The Second Crusade was organized in 1147 to defend Jerusalem. One woman who went on this crusade was Eleanor of Aquitaine, the queen of France. Stories tell of her dressed in red boots and a white cloak, riding a white horse and waving a sword. She was trying to encourage other women to join her on the crusade.

Eleanor started out on the crusade with a huge following. She took trunks full of clothes, jewelry, cooking utensils, carpets, and washbasins, all in a long line of wagons.

At the beginning of the journey, the weather was fine. It was like a wonderful holiday. As they got closer to the Holy Land, they suffered thirst, hunger, and disease just as the first crusaders had. They were also attacked by

Defeated Crusaders

Muslims, and many people were killed. The king narrowly escaped death during this battle.

After a year, Eleanor and her followers arrived in Antioch, their clothes worn out and smelly. They attacked the city of Damascus but failed to capture it. They returned home by sea, which was the fastest possible route.

Battle Shy

Actually battles in medieval times didn't happen all that often. If an army lost a battle, the cost could be very high. Many soldiers could be killed, and important lands could be lost. The morale of the

morale: The way people feel about the life they are leading or the situation they are in.

51

soldiers could get very low. As shown in the Battle of Hastings, the loss of a single battle could mean that a whole country was defeated. In those days, the king actually fought out on the battlefield with his troops. The enemy would be trying very hard to capture or kill him. Nobody wanted the king to be placed at risk. Even some of the cleverest army commanders only fought battles when there was no other choice.

Siege Warfare

Instead of fighting to capture a town or a castle, sometimes armies used a plan of attack called a siege. First, they killed or stole all of the animals. Then they burned the crops around the castle or town. This left the enemy with no food. The army then camped outside the gates of the castle or town while the people inside slowly starved. Usually they surrendered. This way, victory was gained with very few fighting men lost. A siege could take up to several months to work.

Over or Under?

The armies also built wooden siege towers that they wheeled up to the castle walls. Soldiers climbed up them to get over the walls. Another method was to tunnel under the walls, either to gain entry or to make the walls fall down.

Knights had nothing to do with the siege. They just waited either for the enemy to surrender or for the ordinary soldiers to break a hole in the wall. Then they would storm into the castle and fight.

The Hundred Years' War

The Hundred Years' War was, as you might have guessed, a war that lasted for about a hundred years. This war was between France and England. It lasted from 1337 to 1453, though there were times of truce throughout. The French king had died without leaving a son to take his place. One of the reasons for the war was disagreement about who should be the next king. The French noblemen wanted the dead king's nephew to take the crown. But the dead French king had a grandson, the English King Edward III. Edward believed that he should be the new king.

truce: When two groups agree to stop fighting for a period of time.

France's army was much bigger than England's, yet France was losing the Hundred Years' War. The French knights had failed against the English, losing a number of important battles. However, the French eventually drove the English out of France. It was a 17-year-old girl who changed the course of the war.

Saintly Voices

There are records of a number of women fighting in armies during the Middle Ages. The most famous was Joan of Arc.

Joan was born in 1412, one of five children of a poor French farmer. She spent her childhood working on her family's farm. She was a very religious girl who believed that saints talked to her. They told her that it was her mission to free France from the English. The saints also told her to cut off her hair, find some weapons, and dress like a man.

Joan of Arc

Joan could not read or write, and she knew nothing about warfare. Somehow she managed to convince the commander of the French army to take her to Charles. Charles was the man who the French believed belonged on the throne of France.

Woman Warrior

Joan convinced Charles that she should lead an army against the English. Charles gave her a suit of white armor. She led French soldiers in a battle to save the town of Orleans. She was wounded, but she kept fighting. Her bravery inspired her soldiers, and they drove the English away. She fought in more battles and won back land that the English had taken. The

Knight of King Charles VII

English were so afraid of her that many ran away from the battlefield when she approached.

Joan of Arc changed the course of the Hundred Years' War in favor of the French. When Charles was crowned King Charles VII of France, she sat in a place of honor by his side.

Abandoned Heroine

Joan helped France win the Hundred Years' War, but she did not live to be honored for her deeds. She was captured by her enemies and sold to the

English. They decided that she must have used sorcery to defeat them. They accused her of witchcraft and of wearing men's clothes, which was a sin in those days. After 14 months of imprisonment and questioning, she was burned at the stake in 1431. She was 19 years old. King Charles had done nothing to try and save her.

sorcery: The practice of magic, especially black magic, which is supposed to use evil forces to cause harm.

Chapter 4: Introduction

Imagine . . .

you are a young girl serving a queen held captive in a tower by an evil prince.

T HE QUEEN seemed to be getting sadder every day. Vivian tried hard to cheer up her mistress.

"It is such a beautiful day," she said. "Come and sit by the window, my lady. Let me comb your hair."

But the queen refused her offer and stayed in the shadows with her own thoughts. Vivian didn't blame her for being miserable. The poor queen had been locked in the tower for months, prisoner of the evil Prince Méléagant.

As Vivian looked out the window, she noticed a crowd of people gathering. The crowd was on the other side of the dangerous river that cut off the tower. She looked closer.

The eyes of the crowd were on one person, a knight.

"Come and look, madam," cried Vivian. "There is a strange knight. Perhaps he has come to rescue you."

This brought Queen Guinevere to her feet and to the window. It was too far away to tell who the knight was, but Vivian heard the queen catch her breath. She felt sure she knew the knight.

"He cannot rescue me unless he crosses the Sword Bridge," said the queen. "And no one has ever done that."

It was true. The bridge that crossed the raging river was not like any other bridge Vivian had ever seen. It consisted of one long sword blade tied to a tree trunk on each bank. It was as long as two spears, and its edge was as sharp as a razor. Anyone who tried to cross would need armor stronger than any known. Otherwise they would be cut to shreds. But the mysterious knight was standing on the other side of the river, taking off his armor. He approached the bridge with bare hands and feet. Vivian could hear the people as they begged the knight not to continue.

The queen and Vivian clutched at each other for support as they watched. The knight crawled out onto the bridge. His hands and knees were immediately slashed by the bridge, but he crawled on. The knight did not seem to feel any pain. Blood poured from fresh wounds every time he inched forward.

The people watching had now fallen silent. There was no sound apart from the rushing of the deadly river. The knight crawled on. After what seemed like an age, he reached the other side. When he stood up, his hands, feet, arms, and legs were covered in deep gashes cut right to the bone. His wounds were streaming with a large amount of blood. It seemed impossible that he had enough left within his body to keep him standing.

But the knight's ordeal wasn't over. Prince Méléagant came out of the tower and challenged him. Though the knight should have rested in bed for a month to heal his wounds, he accepted the challenge. Someone brought him armor and a horse. Within minutes the two knights were charging at each other. They clashed together with a sound like thunder. It was with such force that their lances broke and their shields shattered to pieces. They were both knocked from their horses.

They continued to fight on foot. Their sword strokes were so violent that they cut through mail and armor. The unknown knight fought strongly, but because of his wounds from the bridge, he didn't have much strength. His sword strokes weakened. The queen, watching from above, knew, as everyone else did, that the knight would not survive the fight.

"Who is this knight, madam?" asked Vivian. "He fights for you, I'm certain. If he knew you were watching, he might find new strength. Call his name."

But the queen was so overcome, she could not call out the knight's name. She was barely able to whisper it to the serving girl. The girl kept her wits though. She heard the name. She leaned out of the window and called as loud as she could.

"Lancelot! Lancelot!" The wounded knight looked up, saw his queen, and found new strength. . . .

Chapter 4

Literary Legends

THE STORY you've just read is about Lancelot, one of the Knights of the Round Table. He did win the fight and rescue the queen. He is perhaps the most well-known knight in literature.

Storytellers

To pass the time when they weren't fighting, knights liked to listen to stories. There weren't a lot of books around in medieval times, and many knights couldn't read anyway. In those days there were special people whose job it was to tell stories. They were called minstrels.

The stories were not like the stories we read. They were written in poetry and usually sung. Knights liked to hear stories about only one thing—other knights.

Knight-Poets

Some knights in southern France decided not to spend their lives fighting. Instead they decided to write poetry and earn a living performing it. They were called troubadours. Their poems weren't about war but about love. The poems were still about knights, but the knights were usually longing for the love of a lady. The lady was always out of their reach. She was either too rich and high-born, or she was already married to someone else.

Each troubadour had a patron. The patron would invite the troubadour to perform poetry at his castle. In return, the troubadour would receive payment. Sometimes the patron asked the troubadour to write poems especially for him.

Bertran de Born was one of the most famous troubadours. He lived at the end of the 12th century and wrote about war as well as love.

King Arthur

In the 12th century, another sort of story became popular with French knights. This time it was about the deeds of an Englishman. This man was King Arthur. The stories were all about Arthur and his knights who lived in wonderful castles. Guinevere was Arthur's wife, and Lancelot was one of his

patron: A person who gives strong support.

knights. Once again the storytellers updated the stories. King Arthur was supposed to have lived in the sixth century. This was hundreds of years before knights appeared and before Englishmen were building castles. The stories were told as if Arthur lived in medieval times.

Knights loved the stories of Arthur so much that they kept listening to them for the next 250 years! The stories were translated into every European language.

Over the years, writers added to the original Arthur stories. One French writer who did this was called Chrétien de Troyes. He introduced the character of Lancelot and called the place where Arthur lived Camelot. He also added magical things to the stories, such as dragons, giants, and enchanted castles.

The story at the beginning of this chapter is based on Chrétien de Troyes's story of Lancelot.

Knight Errant

A knight errant was a knight who wandered around the country by himself. He was looking for ways to prove his courage. He spent his time rescuing damsels in distress and helping the poor. Such knights first appeared in the stories of

Chrétien de Troyes. They were nothing like real-life knights who were busy protecting towns, castles, and even countries. The knights in de Troyes's stories weren't concerned about looking after land or growing crops to feed their families. They were just looking for adventure.

Knights' Ladies

Women were not included in the older knights' tales. The stories were all about the man's world of war. Although the Arthurian tales were about fighting, they were different. Women played an important part in those stories.

In Arthurian stories, the ladies had a lot of control over the knights. They could command the knights to perform deeds to prove their love. In literature, knights weren't fighting to win battles and gain land. They were trying to show the ladies how brave and skilled they were.

The Lady of the Lake

Sometimes, women gave advice to knights. A mysterious woman called the Lady of the Lake instructed Lancelot when he was a young man. She told him how knights should behave.

"A knight must be merciful, kind-hearted, liberal, just, and fearless. Shame must be harder for him to bear than death. The knight must possess two hearts, one as soft as wax, one as hard as a diamond."

She also explained that each piece of the knight's equipment had a meaning. His double-edged sword showed that he had to protect both religion and the people. Even his horse had a symbolic meaning. It represented the people. As the knight led his horse, so he also had to lead the people.

Printed Books

Printing was introduced in Europe in the middle of the 15th century. Suddenly books were available to ordinary people. They were written in the people's language, too, not in Latin. More and more versions of the Arthur story were written, as well as other knightly tales. They were more popular than ever.

Although it was mostly men who wrote books in the Middle Ages, there were some women who wrote. Christine de Pisan, an Italian woman, was a writer in the 15th century. Her book was called *The Book of Three Virtues*. It was about all of

just: Act fairly and properly.

the things a lady must do to manage her household, such as making cloth.

"She, her daughters, and attendants will make cloth, separating the wool, sorting it out, and putting the fine strands aside to make cloth for her husband and herself, or to sell. The thick strands will be used for the small children, her serving women, and the workmen."

Another woman writer was Anna Comnena, the daughter of the emperor of Constantinople. She wrote her father's life story in 15 books. She also wrote about the time of the First Crusade, describing the events she saw there.

Lady Knights

Women in literature began to change. They didn't just sit around waiting to be rescued by knights. They got involved in the adventures as well. Some put on armor and went out to fight their own battles as lady knights.

A book called *Jerusalem Delivered*, based on the story of the First Crusade, was written in 1575. One of the characters was Clorinda, a female

Constantinople: An old name for Istanbul, a large city in Turkey.

pagan warrior. She fell in love with one of her enemies, Tancred, a young crusader knight from Sicily. During a night raid on the crusaders, she wore black armor. This was so that her enemies wouldn't see her. Unfortunately, Tancred didn't recognize Clorinda in the darkness and killed her.

The Faerie Queene, a poem written in 1590 by Edmund Spenser, was based on the story of St. George. In the poem, the knight, St. George, saved Princess Una from the dragon of sin. One of the heroines of *The Faerie Queene* was Britomart. She was a woman who had magic armor and an unbeatable sword.

More About St. George

Along with Arthur and his followers, St. George was also a famous knight in myths and legends. He was best known for killing dragons.

Although he is the patron saint of England, George was actually born in Cappadocia in what is now Turkey. He was an elected officer in the Roman army. But unlike most Romans, he was a Christian. When the Romans banned Christianity, he refused to

pagan: A name Christians use for people who are not Christians.

give up his faith. The Romans beheaded him. Churches were built in his honor in later years.

The crusaders learned about St. George when they traveled to the Holy Land. They were inspired by his story because he was a soldier like them. Some of them saw visions of him while they attacked the cities of Antioch and Jerusalem. They believed the saint helped them to win. The crusaders took their stories back to England, and St. George became a popular saint there.

So What About the Dragons?

St. George died in 303 A.D. However, his dragon-killing exploits weren't added to his story until 600 years later. He was supposed to have killed a dragon in Silene in Libya. According to the legend, this dragon was terrorizing the people and poisoning the countryside with its breath. People gave the dragon sheep to eat. But the dragon got sick of eating sheep and demanded young women to eat instead. Every day a young woman was tied to a rock, and the dragon would come and eat her. They'd just about run out of young women. It was the Princess Sabra's turn to be sacrificed to the monster.

Luckily, St. George happened to ride by, and he killed the dragon and saved the princess. He is

supposed to have killed dragons in England as well. This is unlikely since he never went anywhere near England.

St. George appears in many paintings, stained glass windows, and sculptures. He is usually shown on horseback, wearing armor, and killing a dragon with a lance. Like many of the knights' heroes, George died centuries before knights appeared or armor was invented. But knights preferred that their heroes look exactly like them.

Imagine . . .

you're a squire at a tournament with your knight.

EDMUND WIPED the sweat from his brow and stood back to admire his work. Samson's coat shone like black satin. He combed the horse's mane and tail, then carefully braided them. Through each braid, he placed blue and gold ribbons. Samson switched his tail slowly as if he was aware of how beautiful he looked.

Next, Edmund went to get the caparison and placed it over Samson's back. It was gorgeous: brilliant blue cloth covered with golden lions. Three lions on a blue shield was Sir Richard's coat of arms.

Edmund positioned the saddle correctly on Samson's back. The leather was polished to a rich red-brown. The buckles gleamed. He had been polishing until well after midnight the night before. This morning he had risen before dawn to brush the horse. But it had all been worth it. Samson looked magnificent.

"I don't want you getting in the way at the field," Sir Richard said to Edmund. "Stay away from the arena."

Edmund climbed up onto the inn roof where he could get a good view. He did not want to miss any of the events.

Three hundred knights rode in a row to the arena. Each one wore his own colors on his surcoat and shield. Each horse wore matching colors. The sunlight glinted off swords and armor.

It took Edmund a full five minutes to find Sir Richard's lion crest among the knights. There he was on Samson, who, even from this distance, looked like the best horse on the field. Edmund felt very proud.

The knights came to a halt in front of the spectators' stand and paraded before the ladies.

Edmund saw Sir Richard bow toward the stand. He couldn't make her out himself, but he knew his master had caught sight of Lady Joan. Sir Richard touched the gold embroidered scarf tied to his arm. It belonged to Lady Joan. He was her champion.

The trumpets sounded. The noise of the crowd hushed. The heralds announced the first two teams who were to fight. Each team consisted of 30 knights. Everyone leaned forward waiting for the action to begin.

The two teams lined up at opposite ends of the field. The trumpets sounded again. The peace was broken as the knights spurred on their horses and thundered toward each other. The clash of lances splintering on shields and the shouting of men added to the noise.

If there was any order to the fighting after that, Edmund couldn't see it. Knights charged at other knights without any plan or system. They would shout at each other and clash their weapons. Horses reared, others fell heavily, and some were wounded or even killed.

The sun went behind dark clouds that appeared suddenly out of the east. Before long, heavy rain was pouring down. The soil, which had been kicked up by the horses, turned to mud. Knights who were unhorsed fell to the ground and were covered in sticky mud. They had to struggle to their feet and fight hand to hand with swords.

The scene was one of complete confusion. Edmund lost sight of Sir Richard in the mass of horses and men. There were many knights that used the colors blue and gold. Sometimes he thought he saw Sir Richard but realized it was another knight.

When the fight was over, Edmund had no idea who had won. He ran among the exhausted knights coming off the field until at last he found Sir Richard. His shield was in pieces, his armor dented, and his lion crest crushed. He was also in pain. He had been unhorsed and trampled by his opponent's horse. His armor had saved him from serious injury, but Edmund suspected he had broken several ribs.

Worst of all, even though the tournament had been fought with blunt lances and unsharpened blades, Samson was wounded. The horse had run into the sharp splinters of a broken lance. The mud on his flank was mixed with blood.

Edmund led the wounded horse back to their tent. This was only the first contest. There would be three more days of jousting. . . .

Chapter 5
Tournaments and Chivalry

FIGHTING COMPETITIONS between knights are called tournaments. In times of peace, knights had to keep fit and make sure that their fighting skills didn't get rusty. The knights serving a lord could practice swordplay with each other. But what they really needed was something that was more like the conditions in a real battle. They also needed experience in fighting together as a team. Knights from neighboring areas took part in tournaments.

Tournaments appeared around the end of the 11th century. At first they had very few rules. A tournament took place across an expanse of open countryside. Two teams of knights would fight each other, riding over peasants' fields, across rivers, and around farm buildings. This kind of tournament, with large numbers of knights (sometimes hundreds), was called a mêlée. There were no spectators to watch the activities at the early tournaments.

Dangerous Games

The aim wasn't to kill the opponent but to disarm and capture him. Sometimes the losing knight then had to give his horse and armor to the winner. Knights saw that tournaments were a good way to earn money. If they won, they could sell the armor and horses that they claimed from the defeated knights. Sometimes they held the captured knight for ransom. His lord then had to pay a sum of money to get him back. For the losing knights, it was a very expensive business!

Although knights in tournaments didn't intend to kill each other, accidental death and injury were common. Over time, tournaments were made safer. They were held in fenced-off areas called lists. Rules were introduced, and blunt weapons were used. The tournament in the story about Edmund was one of these safer types.

Jousting

Knights liked the idea of fighting in single combat like the knights in books. When they fought in battles and tournaments, they were just part of a team. If they fought one-on-one, the knight who won kept all of the glory for himself.

In the 13th century, jousts were introduced. These were competitions at tournaments in which only two knights fought. The aim of a joust was to knock the other knight off his horse. The two knights charged at each other with their lances. There was a scoring system. A knight got one point for hitting his opponent above the waist. He received two points for breaking his lance on his opponent's helmet or shoulder. He got three points for knocking his opponent off his horse.

Church Disapproval

Church officials didn't think knights should be fighting each other in tournaments. Even with the rules, they thought that far too many knights were being killed. At one tournament in the town of Neuss in Germany, 60 knights were killed. The Church banned tournaments in Europe between 1130 and 1316. In spite of this, tournaments continued to be held in some places.

Kings of Chivalry

King Edward I of England loved tournaments. He was a tall man and a great warrior. He wore fantastic clothing and rode a black horse. With his long blond hair, he must have looked like a knight

right out of an Arthurian tale. He held his
own tournaments and took part in
them himself. He loved the stories
of King Arthur. In 1284, he even
made a round table for his knights
to sit at.

King Henry II of France also took
part in tournaments. He wasn't as
successful as the English king,
though. In 1559, he held a
tournament to celebrate the marriages of his sister
and his daughter. King Henry fought well all day.
He decided he would have one final joust with the
captain of the royal guard. When the two men
charged, their lances struck each other. The
captain didn't lower his in time, though, and the
lance pierced the king's visor. He died of the
wound a few days later.

How to Host a Tournament

Another king was so interested in tournaments that
he decided to write a book about them. He was
René of Anjou, a French duke who was crowned
king of Jerusalem and Sicily. He held a number of
very expensive tournaments in France.

His book, written around 1460, is called *King
René's Tournament Book*. It describes the armor

knights should wear at a tournament and how they should display their colors. It also tells how the tournament area should be constructed and what the judges should do. Here are some of his instructions for giving the signal to start a battle.

". . . the king of arms should cry, by the order of the judges, taking three great breaths and three great pauses, 'Cut the cords, and begin the battle when you wish.' And after the third cry has been made, those who are to cut the cords should cut them. And at once those who carry the banners, and the foot servants, and those on horseback should shout the cries of each of their tourneying masters. Then the two sides should gather together and fight until by the order of the judges the trumpets sound the retreat."

Knights' Rules

Knights made rules for proper knightly behavior. These rules were very similar to the ones mentioned in the famous stories. As well as being brave in battle, knights had to be compassionate and generous. They also had to behave politely to women. This code became known as chivalry.

compassionate: Feeling sorrow or pity for the suffering of others.

The most important rule of chivalry was to take care of women in need. Men who were rude to women were not permitted to take part in tournaments.

Chivalry Manuals

Manuals, such as *The Book of Chivalry*, outlined the rules of knighthood. Some of these rules and instructions were very similar to those described by the Lady of the Lake. These were told in the fictional story of Lancelot.

Even in war, knights liked to behave properly. If they captured enemy knights, they didn't kill them but held them for ransom. The prisoner knights were treated very well and ate alongside their captors.

Remember William Marshal?

You read about William Marshal in Chapter 2. He had a very successful career after learning his lesson well in that first battle. He knew how important it was to defeat the enemy and to take his horse and armor. In his first tournament, he captured several knights and took their horses as his prize. In one ten-month period late in the 12th century, he reportedly defeated 103 knights in tournaments. He was so successful that he was made knight in charge of nine-year-old King Henry III.

Ladies' Favors

People started to enjoy watching tournaments, and stands were built for the spectators to sit in. Ladies became more involved but not in the fighting. Just as in the stories, the knights fought to impress the ladies.

Each lady would have a favorite knight. He would tie her scarf to his arm to show that he was her knight.

The knights paraded in front of the ladies before the fight began. Sometimes, the ladies would be the judges of the tournament.

Imagine . . .

you are a young peasant boy who lives in France in 1346.

Gaspard sat in a ditch by the side of the road. He watched quietly as the French army marched by. There were so many of them—thousands and thousands of foot soldiers and at least 5,000 knights. How Gaspard envied those knights. They were on their way to win another battle for France. He was only a poor peasant, so he could never be a knight. If ever he fought for France, it would be as a foot soldier.

It was late in the afternoon, but Gaspard wanted to stay just a little longer. From where he was, he could hear the soldiers with crossbows complaining that they were too tired to fight. They had been marching all day. The strings of their crossbows were loose because of the rain. No one, however, was paying any attention to them.

Gaspard decided it was time for him to return home. Just then, the English army appeared like magic in front of the French. They must have been resting in the long grass, and then all stood up suddenly. A flock of black crows took off from a nearby tree, disturbed by the activity. The birds swooped low over the French troops. It crossed Gaspard's mind that it was a bad sign, but then he looked back at the English. How few they were alongside the French! How stupid they must be to think they had any chance of winning!

Gaspard realized that he was surrounded by soldiers. He could not get out of the ditch without being seen. He would have to stay where he was until the soldiers moved onto the battlefield. The sound of shouted orders could be heard along the lines of soldiers. The grumbling crossbowmen pulled back the strings of their weapons, ready to fire.

Gaspard realized with a thud of his heart that he was on the battlefield!

The crossbowmen leaped in the air and yelled as they moved forward, trying to startle their enemy. The Englishmen stood still. The crossbowmen leaped and yelled again, and then did the same for a third time. The English did not move a muscle. The crossbowmen let go a set of arrows. Some of the arrows found their target, and English soldiers fell to the ground. The crossbowmen stopped to reload their weapons. It was then that the English bowmen all took one step forward and aimed their bows. They fired and fired again with such speed that it seemed as if arrows were falling like rain.

Many of the crossbowmen fighting for the French were killed or wounded. The rest dropped their crossbows, turned, and ran. When the French knights saw the bowmen running, they were so angry that they attacked the bowmen themselves. The knights cursed them for their cowardice. While the French knights were busy killing their own men, the English archers continued to fire.

The sun, hidden from view all day, suddenly appeared below the dark clouds. The sunlight shone right in the eyes of the French. They could hardly see their enemies. With their backs to the setting sun, the English could see their enemies more easily.

Shower after shower of arrows fell on the French knights. They were not aimed at the knights themselves but at their horses. Many brave warhorses died, pierced with arrows.

Darkness fell, and Gaspard could see no more. But he could hear the terrible sounds of swords clashing and arrows whistling through the air. Men were groaning and dying all around him. It was horrible. At around midnight he was finally able to make a dash back to his home. That night any dreams he had about becoming a knight, or at least a valiant foot soldier, disappeared. He thanked God that he was born the son of a poor peasant. . . .

Chapter 6
End of an Era

THE BATTLE OF CRÉCY in 1346 was one of the many battles that the French lost during the Hundred Years' War. The French army consisted of more than 40,000 men. The English only had 13,000, most of whom were foot soldiers. The English won because they were extremely organized. The French knights lost because they were overconfident. Also, they could not rely on the Italian crossbowmen they had paid to fight with them. Here is the way Sir Jean Froissart described how the crossbowmen were overcome by the English archers.

"Then the English archers stepped forth one pace and let fly their arrows so wholly and so thick that it seemed snow. When the Genoways felt the arrows piercing through heads, arms, and breasts, many of them cast down their crossbows and did cut their strings and return discomfited."

Genoways: People from the Italian city of Genoa.

discomfited: Defeated in battle.

Anti-Knight Weapons

Things were not going as well for knights as they had in earlier centuries. Knights discovered that they weren't invincible. The weapons used against knights were simple, but army commanders had learned ways to use them effectively. One foot soldier with a bow and arrow was no match for a charging knight. However, a line of bowmen could be deadly.

Longbows and Crossbows

Longbows were first used in Wales in the 12th century. Six-and-a-half feet in height, they were bigger than the bows that had been used before. They could shoot arrows a distance of 1,000 feet. The shafts of the arrows were made from the wood of yew trees. The feathers on the arrows, called flights, were from geese. If the archers were shooting at infantrymen or horses, they used arrows with barbed metal heads. For shooting at knights, they used sharp metal points called bodkins to pierce the armor.

invincible:
Incapable of
being defeated.

Crossbows were even more deadly. They shot arrows further and at greater speed than longbows. The crossbow had a metal bow fixed to a central wooden stock. The bowstring had to be pulled back to load the arrow. The arrows were called quarrels and were made of steel. To load his crossbow, the archer had to rest it on the ground and use both hands. Or he had to wind the bowstring back with a handle. This made loading slow, so the crossbowman couldn't shoot as many arrows as the longbowman.

Pikes

A pike is a long stick with a sharp metal point on the end. It was used very successfully against knights. The foot soldiers stood very close together with their pikes pointing out like a porcupine. The knights couldn't get close enough to use their weapons.

Polearms

Weapons on long poles were developed that could pierce and cut a knight's armor like can openers. A poleax was a three-in-one weapon with an ax head, a spike, and a hammer on the end. Another similar weapon was the halberd, which had an ax head, a spear, and a spike or a hook. With this weapon, a skilled man could hook a knight off his horse, then stab or chop him.

Falling Fortunes

By the 15th century, young men no longer wanted to become knights. It was expensive and dangerous. People didn't think so highly of knights anymore. In battle, they were no more important than ordinary soldiers, who now also wore armor and rode horses. Young men who did become knights were more interested in going to tournaments than going to war.

When William the Conqueror was king of England, there were 5,000 knights in the country. Two hundred years later, this number had gone down to less than 400. King Henry III had to force men to take up arms and become knights.

Blood Sport

Tournaments became sporting events, more for entertainment than for battle practice. They were held to celebrate weddings and other special events. Knights wore expensive clothes and draped their horses in brightly colored robes. Even their armor became highly decorated with finely detailed patterns.

Tournaments became theatrical events. Knights dressed up and played the part of their favorite character from the Arthurian legends. Everyone wore costumes, including the ladies and the minstrels. There was music and dancing.

One particularly lavish tournament was held in 1520 near Calais. As a gesture of friendship between France and England, the kings of both countries jousted each other.

The kings, knights, and horses all wore clothing made of gold cloth. Tents, made of rich materials with gold thread, were set up for eating and dancing. The tournament became known as the Field of Cloth of Gold.

A 15th-Century Knight

Pas d'Armes

Knights now preferred fighting for sport to fighting for war. They started to live in a fantasy world. In the 15th century, a popular exhibition was the *pas d'armes*, or feat of arms. Such an event would go on for weeks. This was a different kind of joust where a knight would defend a piece of road or a bridge. Then he would invite other knights to oppose him.

In the Feat of the Fountain of Tears, a French knight, Jacques de Lalaing, defended a fountain. It was

lavish:
Expensive
and richly
decorated.

91

of a unicorn with a lady whose eyes ran with tears. He defended the fountain for a whole year, fighting off 22 challengers.

Other knights made extravagant vows. A knight might vow not to sleep in a bed until he had performed a special feat of arms. One knight, Suero de Quiñones, vowed to wear an iron collar and chain around his neck. He did this every Thursday until he had taken part in a feat of arms.

The Dark Side

There were still knights who made a living by fighting, but not many were employed by lords. Unemployed knights, called Free Companies, rode around Europe hiring themselves out to any country that would pay. Some of them seemed to forget all about chivalry. If there were no wars, they wandered around the countryside threatening peasants unless they paid them money. Once again, knights had become lawless and rough.

Fire Power

In the 14th century, an amazing new weapon was introduced—the gun. At first, handguns were very unreliable and likely to blow up in the user's face. Also, gunpowder was very expensive.

Guns played a part in the downfall of knights. They began to be used as the main weapons in battles. By the end of the 15th century, knights were not needed anymore—any soldier could fire a gun.

Knights had plenty of other things to keep them busy, though. In addition to taking care of their own lands, they became involved in local government. Instead of settling disputes by fighting, knights helped settle them in courts of law.

Modern Knights and Ladies

There are still knights today, but they don't wear armor and fight with swords. In Great Britain, the queen gives knighthoods each year. A knighthood is a special reward given to a person for performing exceptional service for their country. Men who are knighted put the title "Sir" before their names. "Dame" is the title used by knighted women.

There are no knights in shining armor anymore, but they continue to be popular in books and films. More than a thousand years after knights first appeared, people still love stories about them and their ladies.

Where to from Here?

You've just read about how knights and ladies lived during medieval times. Here are some ideas for learning more about knights and medieval life.

The Library

Some books you might enjoy include:
- *A Medieval Castle* by Fiona Macdonald
- *Knights in Armor* edited by John D. Clare
- *Medieval Knights* by David Nicolle
- *Medieval Life* by Andrew Langley
- *The Age of Knights and Castles* by World Book Staff

TV, Film, and Video

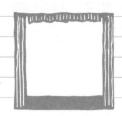

Watch TV listings for Public Broadcasting Station (PBS) programs on the Middle Ages. Check your local video store or library for films about knights, lords, and ladies.
Some suggestions are:
- *Knights and Armor*
- *Crossbow*

The Internet

Search the Internet using keywords such as *medieval knights*, *chivalry*, *medieval armor*, and *castles*.

People and Places

Museums often have collections that include medieval artifacts such as armor, weapons, and tapestries. Visit these museums to see for yourself how knights lived.

The Ultimate Fiction Book

Be sure to check out *Bertrand's Quest*, the companion volume to *A Knight's Journey*. *Bertrand's Quest* tells the story of a boy who is determined to become a knight. This story is based on the real life adventures of Bertrand du Guesclin.

Decide for yourself
where fact stops
and fiction begins.

Index